THE
SHUT-
INS

Armand
Di Francesco

Our Sunday Visitor, Inc.
Huntington, Indiana 46750

Cover design by James McIlrath

Library of Congress Catalogue No.: 84-62171
ISBN: 0-87973-599-6

Printed in the United States of America

599

This book is dedicated to my daughter,

Patricia Elina Di Francesco
1955 — 1977

The following prayer, written by Patricia, was found amongst her writings shortly after she passed into the presence of the Lord:

"I pray that if I die tomorrow, I'm happy to go. I want to be with my Creator and to serve Him. I'm happy I loved today, was loved, and I'm truly sorry for any wrongs I've done and ask for guidance to be shown the right way. Let me only give love in its purest, most truthful form, and let me be able to distinguish it from my 'self.' If I die tonight, I will have died loving God for showing me the things in my heart I could not interpret. I must love all people and be deceptive to no one. Whether these feelings are ego-centered, making myself an angel, or whether they are sincere in the Lord's foundation of right and wrong, I ask help to be shown the Way. Show me myself so I can live the life given me with your soul's desire, for I am an extension of your Grace and want to be worthy. You share so much beauty with me. If I die tonight, I lived another of many timeless days, whether sorrowful or full of joy, with the appreciation and awareness of my being. I ask for a little understanding of what is true to my heart rather than my conscience, and to be understood by others. Let me see more clearly with my mind, not only my eyes. I strive for truth. Don't let me get lost. I feel your Love in so many senses. Let me reflect it."

TABLE OF CONTENTS

INTRODUCTION

THE 20th century is remarkable because of the unprecedented increase in the number and proportion of older people over the age of 65. Due to the tremendous medical, social and technological advances, there are now approximately 25 million Americans in this group, with the figure expected to double early in the next century. Twelve percent are shut-ins, individuals who for the most part are confined to their homes or flats. They are the "forgotten Americans," withdrawn from the mainstream of life, "out of sight and out of mind." Once part of the pillars of their communities, they now are generally ignored in a society that idealizes and glorifies youth and achievement.

Shut-ins are of many varieties, but chiefly their afflictions are such that they are forced to be housebound with a varying degree of limitations on living and functioning. About 12% of those over 65 years of age are shut-ins, including 5% who reside in nursing homes. Another

1

two million shut-ins have physical or mental handicaps that confine them and significantly impair their lifestyle. Moreover, seven million of our elderly are poor, with at least one-third having an annual income in the neighborhood of $2,000. Forced to live in ghettoes and slums, it is no wonder that many suffer from depression and loneliness, dejection and abandonment, feeling separated and alienated from others.

It has been said that the degree of civilization of any nation or society is based on their treatment of their aged, elderly and handicapped citizens. On this basis, America's attitude leaves much to be desired. In contrast, great civilizations, such as the Egyptians and Chinese, had profound respect for their elders for centuries. The Romans gained world power and renown through the mature guidance of their elderly rulers and senators. Growing old and infirm in America, on the other hand, involves an increasing lack of respect, relegation to being treated like children, being ignored or entertained with indifference.

The problems of shut-ins are physical, emotional and economic. Of these, the loss of mobility, of hearing and sight, of independence, have the greatest impact. They are more prone to loneliness and depression. Their handicaps generate more anxiety, frustration and stresses of diminished activities with little to look forward to in life. With the loss of resources and decreased mastery in coping with life's problems, feelings of helplessness and a decreasing sense of purpose aggravate their invalidism and personal sufferings. Shut-ins suffer and have to endure more than others because of their increased deprivation.

Harry Emerson Fosdick said: "Rebellion against your handicaps gets you nowhere. Self-pity gets you nowhere. One must have the adventurous daring to accept oneself as a bundle of possibilities and undertake the most interesting game in the world . . . making the most

2

of one's best." Life, with all its vicissitudes, is often beyond comprehension and, like Cardinal Newman in his prayer, we must say: "I know not what purpose I have in life, but He knows." We have within us the power to overcome our fears and misfortunes and to make our lives more meaningful in spite of our handicaps. It is my hope that this book will contribute to all shut-ins an understanding of their problems and guidance in dealing with them.

Armand Di Francesco, M.D.

1

THE STRUGGLE FOR INDEPENDENCE

SIXTY-FIVE years ago, in the foothills of the Berkshires, a daughter, Mary Patricia, was born to a middle-class Irish family with three strapping sons. Bright and vivacious, attractive and loquacious, Mary Pat grew up destined to make her mark in the world. In college, she graduated magna cum laude with a doctorate in psychology. While in school, she met and married John, an engineering student. They had a good marriage and John was a devoted, admiring husband who respected his wife's strong and independent character. They both worked and shared the rearing of their son and daughter. As a counselor, Mary Pat was dedicated and took pride in helping many people with their problems.

At age 55, Mary Pat came down with cardiac and circulatory problems. Her husband was supportive and, not one to let anything get her down, Mary Pat continued to do some work and to take part in social and cultural activities to the best of her ability. Slowly and insidiously, she found herself to be slowing down, stumbling or losing her balance and developing tremors of her hands. A medical examination revealed that Mary Pat had Parkinson's disease, or paralysis agitans. This is a malady that affects the basal ganglia in the brainstem which influence the pyramidal tract to maintain muscle tone and initiate slow, steady muscle activity. The disease causes muscle weakness, tremors of the hands and head, and muscle rigidity. Other features are a mask-like facial expression, drooling of saliva and an involuntary tendency to speed up while walking.

Her condition progressed to the point of invalidism wherein she required considerable assistance from her husband, who took her to doctors, hospitals and physiotherapy clinics. At home, she stayed in her room and frequently called John to do things for her. Both had looked forward so much to retirement and the enjoyment of travel and pleasurable activities, but their world had turned into a nightmare. John found himself trapped into the role of nursemaid, chief cook and bottle-washer. He lost patience at times and his nerves became frayed as his sleep was interrupted by frequent calls at night to take his wife to the bathroom. John began to rant and rave at her, feeling that she "wasn't doing enough to help herself."

Mary Pat, in turn, felt both hurt and angry at his accusations and developed a reactive depression to her inability to be less dependent. She felt so frustrated and helpless at her loss of efficiency. John came down with ulcers as a result of the mixture of guilt, anxiety and resentment over the situation. Both were unhappy and disconsolate shut-ins, unable to resolve their predicament.

One of the worst situations to deal with, especially for those who had been conscientious, hardworking and independent individuals, is that of loss of being self-sufficient. Laid low by old age and physical infirmities, many find themselves as shut-ins, with a decreased capacity to control their lives and deal with their problems. Shut-ins feel helpless, have lowered self-esteem, lack self-confidence with a loss of purpose and identity. They feel: "What good am I?" and are so ashamed and humiliated. This leads to fear and anger at their situation. Sometimes, invalids, like Mary Pat, desire their mate to care for them much as a parent.

The crux of most marital problems in older people is their handling of the dependency relationship. It is very common for older people to have a fear of dependency. When people are questioned about old age, they often make statements like, "I don't mind it as long as my health is O.K." or "as long as I'm not a burden to anyone." Chiefly it is a loss of health or loss of income that increases dependency needs. These are realistic problems of the shut-in.

There are some individuals who grow up with a neurotic dependency on another for their own sense of self which leads to excessive demands and attempts to control another person. The dependent personality seeks to gain and control a strong "protector." Their self-esteem is based on gaining approval from others and their self-confidence hinges on success in attracting and holding them. They get pleasure only in doing things for others to please and win them over. Often acting like a "martyr," they pretend to be independent, but continue to demand help from others.

While we cannot predict the circumstances of our lives, we do have a choice and we have to take charge of our own lives. We have to honestly face our situations and problems, and live with courage, resourcefulness and dignity to the best of our ability. Many people came to Jesus with problems and His replies often started with a verb of action. We must do something about our difficulties and the turning point of all change is within ourselves. We are responsible for our own actions because no one can save us from bad habits, laziness, greed or

7

lack of virtue. An open, active mind is needed to solve personal problems.

Shut-ins do not have a monopoly on suffering and misery. Everyone has limitations of one sort or another. It is our attitude toward our disability that matters. It is essentially a matter of accepting, coping and forgetting about false pride. A shut-in, depending on his disabilities, shifts from degrees of independence to degrees of dependence. No matter what one's handicap is, there is always something one can do, some talent to develop. A woman in Florida, who has spent years in an iron lung, paralyzed by polio and only able to move her head, designs and draws beautiful greeting cards with a pencil and brush held by her teeth.

Accept your limitations and think of what you can do to help yourself. What you cannot do, ask for help from those around you or from social agencies. Show appreciation and don't be demanding, but ask for help in a dignified and courteous manner. Lord Beaverbrook, in his book *Don't Trust To Luck*, wrote that man "can only keep his judgment intact, his nerves sound and his mind secure by the process of self-discipline." Every stage of life has a purpose in God's plan and the purpose is to live it, to reach out daily and enjoy each new experience. Dr. Norman Vincent Peale stated that too many older people suffered from "psychosclerosis" or "hardening of the enthusiasm." Let us therefore take time out to marvel at a beautiful sunset, listen to a child laughing and enjoy the beauty of flowers. Accept yourself as you are and live, loving God.

2

THE PARADOX OF PAIN AND SUFFERING

Why is man allowed to be born if God is only going to give him a hopeless life of uselessness and frustration? (Job 3:23)

The noble art of medicine was conceived in sympathy and born of necessity when man first cried out in pain. Strangers to no one, pain and suffering are part of the human experience. With the pains of labor, we enter into the world to utter our first cry. Pain and pleasure are really unavoidable, and are the basic regulators of behavior in man and the lower animals. According to Sigmund Freud, the father of psychoanalysis, life is living by the pleasure principle, that is, seeking pleasure and avoiding pain if we can.

The word "pain" is derived from the Latin word *poena*, meaning punishment. We still feel that way at times when we are suffering, and say: "What did I do to deserve this?" Whereas we have considered pain to be our enemy, it has actually been our constant friend, for

9

pain is a signal of alarm and danger, signifying that something is wrong, that the state of harmony and equilibrium in the body has been disturbed. It is nature's warning signal to preserve the body from destruction. It promotes healing by preventing further abuse of a broken bone, burned skin, tired muscles or a weak heart.

Because of its usefulness, we do not want to eliminate pain, but we do want to understand it, how we can benefit from it, and how to control it. However, the constant, unbearable pain of terminal cancer or other disease is something that seems to have no obvious purpose. As R. Melzack said in his book, *Puzzle Of Pain* (Penguin Books), "There is no merit to this suffering, no lesson to be learned." Why some religious martyrs experience ecstasy instead of agony as they were put to death may seem to be paradoxical, just as some individuals have been in the most severe state of pain when no organic cause could be found.

Sensing or feeling pain is a process which involves three areas in the nervous system: nerve receptors, nerve conductors and specific brain areas that integrate the whole experience. Receptors are nerve endings in skin, muscles, joints and organs which are stimulated by anything potentially destructive, such as electrical, mechanical, chemical or temperature extremes. When these receptors are stimulated, nervous impulses go immediately to the spinal cord by nerve conductors. Almost instantaneously, a reflex arc or action takes place with motor nerves being stimulated to produce some type of reflex action designed to protect the "damaged" area. An example would be the sudden pulling-away of a hand upon touching a hot object.

At the same time that this occurs, nervous impulses travel up the spinal cord to the reticular activating system in the brainstem and to the thalamus (feeling center) in the inner brain itself. The brain is put on "red alert" to the danger being presented. An incomparable computer, the brain determines where the pain is, what actions to take to ease the pain, what emotional reaction to feel, what consequences might occur and what steps to take in the future. Since we all are unique individuals with unique inheritances and past experiences, it follows that our reactions to pain may differ in many respects.

Primitive man believed that every ache or stabbing pain was due to a needle, stone, or fire thrust into the body by evil spirits or demons. For over two thousand years, acupuncture has been practiced in the Republic of China for the treatment of pain and as the only form of anesthesia in certain surgical procedures. No one really knows why acupuncture removes pain, and there are many for whom the procedure does not work. Taught in school to Chinese children at an early age, acupuncture no doubt represents a form of classical, cultural conditioning.

What we do know is that everyone has a different threshold and receptivity for pain. About one in 20 Americans lack a normal perception for pain: that is, they either feel no pain, or very little, and thus suffer more injuries than others. Pain researchers at the Massachusetts General Hospital in Boston found a woman who had seven babies without experiencing any labor pains. She had an aunt who died of cancer without pain and two of her children were analgesic and felt no pain.

A strong pain overshadows a weak one, which explains why biting one's lip will provide some relief from a weaker pain elsewhere. Every individual's reaction to pain is based on the type of nervous system inherited and one's personality traits, as well as cultural attitudes. Psychoneurotics show an increased awareness or perception of pain. Many psychotics, paradoxically, may feel no pain when in psychotic states, especially catatonic stupors. It is as if their minds were detached from their bodies. Many cases of "masked" depression present themselves to the family doctor with a chief

11

complaint of a vague, chronic pain for which no physical cause can be found.

In December 1975, John Hughes and Hans Kosterlitz, Scottish neurochemists at the University of Aberdeen, discovered that the brain cells in the central gray matter of the brainstem, called the reticular activating system, contained a substance called enkephalin, the brain's own "morphine." Enkephalin kills pain the same way as morphine, by stimulating the nerve cells that switch off the responses to painful stimuli. Further research may lead not only to a better understanding of drug addiction but also to better control of chronic, intractable pain.

Many shut-ins suffer from painful diseases, such as crippling arthritis, cardiovascular disorders, emphysema and the general debility of the aged. They share and endure pain that is often difficult to bear. Emotionally, they must cope with feelings of meaninglessness, trying to find some purpose in existence. So often, the urge to give up and sink into depression arises. How one reacts to chronic pain is as important as the way that one perceives the pain. Negative emotions such as anger, resentment, guilt feelings and depression only serve to make the condition worse and intensify the pain.

The first rule in dealing with chronic pain is to be relaxed. Relaxation is accomplished by mentally focusing on positive words and images which in turn will lead to positive feelings. I like to close my eyes and imagine myself lying on the warm sand of a beach, gazing up at a brilliantly blue sky, watching soft, billowy clouds floating by as I feel the warm rays of the sun and the gentle breezes wafting by, listening to the gentle lapping of the water. I dwell on that scene for as long as I wish to relax. Perhaps you may have your own peaceful scene that you may wish to use.

Do not dwell on your pain and avoid thinking about it. It only intensifies it. So try changing your thoughts onto something pleasant and distracting. That might be thanking God for His blessings and graces or getting interested in some educational program on television or talking to a cheerful friend.

Avoid feeling guilty or fearful, because these negative feelings, besides being useless, only make the perception of pain worse. Those shut-ins with rigid consciences often interpret their chronic suffering as punishment due to a tendency to have guilt complexes. We can with practice and acceptance learn to live with pain and increase our tolerance to it. Acceptance means facing reality: "I have a condition that causes pain. It is a fact. While I can't change the condition, I can change my attitude toward it. It will ease and I have to learn to live with it and do what I can to minimize it."

Lastly, do not be afraid to discuss your condition with your doctor, who can with the judicious use of analgesics and mood-altering medications make you feel more comfortable.

3

LONELINESS IS THE PITS

DURING my internship at Hamilton General Hospital, while working in the Emergency Room, a frantic call for help came at 2 a.m. Arriving there with the ambulance crew and a police cruiser, I found an elderly lady in her apartment who said: "I'm lonely!" Nonplussed, the officers explained that this situation was a little "above and beyond the call of duty." She asked to be arrested and, when told that she hadn't committed any offense, went outside shrilly screaming to be arrested. She *was* arrested, as a public nuisance, and spent the weekend in jail. On Monday morning, she paid a $25 fine and told the judge that it was cheaper and "more fun" than going elsewhere for company and entertainment!

When Admiral Richard E. Byrd wintered alone on the Antarctic icecap, his purpose was to study weather conditions and to experience solitude. As time went on, he found himself struggling hard against anxiety and loneliness. He wrote: "A man can isolate himself from habits

15

and conveniences, and force his mind to forget. But the body is not so easily sidetracked. It keeps on remembering. Habit has set in the core of its being a system of automatic physiochemical actions and reactions which insist on replenishment. That is where the conflict arises. I don't think a man can do without sounds, smells, voices and touch any more than he can do without phosphorus and calcium."

Loneliness can best be described as an unhappy feeling, or as a depressed, isolated feeling, because of a lack of companionship. Like cattle, human beings have a "herd instinct" that drives them together, and isolation only creates feelings of sadness and melancholy. Bartenders are well aware that the majority of their clientele are there because of loneliness. Many lonely people take the world's oldest tranquilizer, alcohol, to numb their depression, often becoming problem drinkers or alcoholics. The fears of old age and shut-ins are loneliness and poverty. A recurrent theme in contemporary rock music is that of loneliness, as in the Beatles' tune, "Eleanor Rigby . . . look at all the lonely people."

A part of all human existence, loneliness is known by everyone. It is a constant awareness of aloneness, of feeling separate from all human contact, of melancholy gloom and abandonment. Many individuals, including great figures such as President Abraham Lincoln and Frédéric Chopin, have felt alone and lonely even when with friends and those who loved them. The emotional essence of loneliness is very much like that of a reactive depression, that is the sense of loss experienced with the bereavement of a loved one. Little children cling to their parents because they fear being alone. Fear of the dark is a fear of being alone. Sigmund Freud quoted a child who was afraid of the dark as saying: "If someone talks, it gets lighter."

People have found many ways of overcoming loneliness. Organizations exist because of the need for acceptance and human contact. America, it has been said, is a nation of joiners. We join clubs, guilds, fraternities and sororities, lodges and professional groups. These are usually listed in one's obituary. Some people get "sick" and go to hospitals because they are lonely. There are those who are lonely because they can't make contact with others, due to hostile and destructive feelings. They feel threatened by others and fear they cannot perhaps control their own violent impulses. They tend to be seclusive, withdrawn, eccentric or odd in personality.

Poverty may have excluded them from socializing. Even being wealthy and living on "Nob Hill" can create isolation from others. Peculiar religious sects separate themselves from others and induce detached situations. Physical disabilities such as blindness, crippling defects and deformities, deafness and brain damage can segregate individuals from others. What is worse is the distancing of so-called normal persons from the handicapped due to ignorance, fears or a lack of compassion. Children also become lonely when parents who have a nomadic way of life move frequently, such as seasonal workers, military personnel, businessmen or salesmen. It is difficult for these children to establish a feeling of belonging to any group.

Loneliness can be overcome, but it must be done in a healthy way. It requires effort and a desire to do something for others. Everyone is lonely at times and we all feel cut off or alienated from others at some point in our lives. If you are lonely, you have two choices: to feel sorry for yourself and "curse the darkness," or do something positive and constructive about it. Lord Chesterfield told his son that the secret of getting people to like you is to help the other fellow to like himself. You must show him his best side and his good qualities. Help him to feel that you understand him because so many others do not. By becoming interested in others, you gain more friends than by trying to get them interested in you.

17

Do things with others. Get interested in others and get to know others. Sometimes loneliness comes about because of a fear of others and is a form of avoiding getting hurt, but we must make the first move and do something about it. This involves getting acquainted and mixing in with other people. It may be difficult at first, but "familiarity breeds contempt" for these fears. Remember that we are doing God's command when we go out to others and try to spread a little sunshine. It is in loving that we become loved. We can say something nice to three different people each day to develop a habit of kindness. Too many of us do more hurting rather than helping, more putting down than lifting up, more counting of our problems than blessings. It has been said that "the road to hell is paved with good intentions." How many times have you thought of doing something good but didn't? Right now is a good time to start.

4

CONQUER YOUR FEARS WITH COURAGE

FROM the beginning, when primitive man shivered in fear from the awesome and threatening forces of nature and compared his puniness with the infinite power of the universe, human beings have been subject to fear, that emotional state of alarm and impending doom. Fear and anxiety are necessary parts of life, vital to the existence of the individual and the species, for every living creature is continually in danger of destruction. Danger, real or imagined, induces degrees of fear, depending on the size of the situation. Ralph Waldo Emerson, the American poet and philosopher, said: "He has not learned the lesson of life who does not every day surmount a fear."

Fear is healthy when it is based on the recognition of danger at hand, such as a sudden storm while out sailing on a lake. It can be unhealthy when it is due to a misuse of the imagination, causing needless suffering, called anxiety. Anxiety gives one the same physical and psycho-

19

logical signs and symptoms as fear, but the cause is different. For example: while sailing on a lake in calm and sunny weather, you get the thought: "What if a big storm should come up and we capsize and drown?" That thought can induce severe anxiety.

This anticipatory anxiety, or worrying about things before they happen, is commonly experienced by individuals who are pessimistic, negative thinkers, insecure, lack self-confidence, tend to feel guilty (and thus anticipate punishment of some sort) and who lack faith in themselves and in God. They usually have led insecure lives, experiencing fear throughout their growing years.

Our reaction, both physical and mental, to danger is the result of inborn, natural defense mechanisms and by learned patterns of behavior. As soon as we perceive danger, certain chemical changes occur in the body. The adrenal glands, situated above the kidneys, secrete adrenaline in the bloodstream, and the brain amine levels of noradrenaline and dopamine are increased to prepare for "fight or flight" reactions. Adrenaline speeds up the heart, digestion stops and blood is diverted from the abdominal organs to the muscles. Sugar is mobilized as fuel from the liver and noradrenaline makes one alert, attentive and ready for action.

The symptoms of fear and anxiety are a feeling of dread or impending doom, rapid heart rate, tremors, palpitations, perspiration, "knots" in the stomach, fatigue, tension and perhaps nausea and vomiting. No one likes these feelings, and danger is attached to any situation or object or idea that precipitates them. Whenever one gets these symptoms, danger is attached and we then get anticipatory anxiety, that is we fear getting those frightening symptoms again in that situation or with that object or idea. It becomes a phobia.

Panic, on the other hand, is acute and dramatic. It is a sudden and general fright that may be intense and disorganizing. All of us have experienced it at some time in our lives. I had my first panic attack as a freshman in college when I got trapped in a women's rest room by mistake. Panic makes us fear loss of control. Bewilderment, dread, apprehension and a fear of mental collapse pervades our whole being. This may last from a few minutes to an hour. Once the adrenaline is "burned up" these signs and symptoms subside. The symptoms are very distressing, but not dangerous.

Imaginery fear can be contagious. On May 30, 1883, the Brooklyn Bridge was opened. Shortly after, an unreasoning fear swept through the crowd that the bridge was on the point of collapse. How this panic began is not exactly known, but someone said that the bridge began to sway under the weight of the crowd; another said that someone shouted that the bridge was dangerous and a woman screamed when she fell on a flight of steps. In the rush to get off the bridge, 12 people were trampled to death and 25 were seriously injured. If one dwells on what might happen and keeps dwelling on it, a state of fear leading to panic ensues and this precipitates irrational behavior. Elderly people feel secure in familiar and stable surroundings. When they are moved to a strange place, such as a hospital or nursing home, many aged individuals become panicky, confused or agitated because they do not recognize their surroundings, or new faces about them. In this respect their reactions resemble the little child who becomes upset when separated from its parents, and this is one of the reasons that this period is called "second childhood."

Dr. John Schindler, in his book *How To Live 365 Days Of The Year*, gives these principles to make your life richer: Keep life simple; avoid watching for "a knock in your motor"; learn to like work; have a good hobby; learn to be satisfied; like people; say the cheerful, pleasant thing; meet your problems with decision; always be planning something and say "nuts" to irritations.

Excessive worrying is an inordinate concern about oneself and is a form of selfishness. We cannot love others if we get too wrapped up in ourselves. We must learn to change our thoughts and think positively, for there is a good side to everything. There is no need to get a new personality, for it is only a change in attitudes and values that must take place. The amount of change, of course, is proportionate to the amount of effort put into it. Remember what Mark Twain said: "I am an old man and have known a great many troubles, but most of them never happened."

By virtue of their situation, shut-ins have many factors in their lives that can lead to negative thinking and worrying. Loss of efficiency, dependency needs, lack of extended family support and financial problems are all realistic worries. The shut-in, with his idleness, has a veritable "Devil's playground" to develop all sorts of anticipatory anxiety. Dwelling on past sins and mistakes, as well as fearing future calamities, only perpetuates a state of apprehension. Fear of eventual physical or mental collapse is a common worry.

If you catch yourself worrying, change your thoughts and try to think pleasant and positive thoughts. Read Matthew 7:25-34, which ends with: "So don't be anxious about tomorrow. God will take care of your tomorrow too. Live one day at a time." The 17th Psalm of David also provides comfort and reassurance. Remember that God is always with you. When Job's wife (Job 2:9-10) told Job to curse God and die, after being struck with a terrible case of boils, Job replied: "What? Shall we receive only pleasant things from the hand of God and never anything unpleasant?"

The message that Jesus gave is that there is nothing in this world really worth worrying about, and when we put everything (worries) in His hands, we are free to love. When we cultivate the power of love, fears dissipate themselves. Courage comes from the knowledge that we are loved by Him and that we are living for Him and His purpose for us. Too many people dwell on what they can't do instead of dwelling on what they can do. The lesson of Calvary is that we all have a cross of some sort to bear in life, that we all stumble and at times fall under its weight, that sometimes we have to ask a Simon of Cyrene to help us carry it. It may be a doctor, clergyman or friend. And sometimes, you can be a Simon and help others with their burden.

5

UNDERSTANDING DEPRESSION

L IFE is a struggle for survival of body and spirit. The motivating drive for sustenance of the spirit is based on the need for affection, the need for acceptance and the need for approval. In one way or another, we conduct our lives, healthily or unhealthily, to satisfy these needs. When adversity or tragedy strikes, thus limiting our ability to cope or succeed, as in the case of shut-ins, depression sets in. Loneliness, isolation, feeling unneeded and unwanted, suffering and monotony provide the "soil" for the cultivation of a variety of depressions. Every single day there are 14 million cases of depression severe enough to require treatment. Depression is as old as life itself and is part of normal human experience. We all at times have some feelings of sadness and disappointments. It is when depression is deep and prolonged, interfering with our adjustment, that it becomes abnormal.

A few hundred years before Christ, Hippocrates,

the father of medicine, noticed that people had "pendulum moods" with ups and downs. The biblical King Saul suffered from cycles of moods. The composers Peter Tchaikovsky and Jean Sibelius poured their moodiness into their music. The poet Thomson revealed his depressive feelings in his work entitled: "The City Of The Dreadful Night." Abraham Lincoln was prone to fits of melancholy and was saved from being an unhappy failure by the intelligence and decisiveness of his friends, a fact of his life which many do not know. After the death of Ann Rutledge, he was in a deep state of depression for months, unable to do anything.

Depression is a feeling of undue sadness, dejection or melancholy for which there is no apparent or logical external cause. It is a mood that has been experienced as despair, gloom, a feeling of emptiness or feeling "dead inside" and a feeling of foreboding or numbness. It often begins by a loss of appetite and sleep disturbances. Occasionally, it is a problem in falling asleep, but more commonly it is early morning awakening and not being able to go back to sleep. There is also a loss of interest in one's appearance and in one's surroundings. The depressed person doesn't care about going out or seeing anyone, even relatives or friends.

Accompanying depression is a loss of one's sense of humor. Nothing appears to be funny and it is difficult even to smile. Self-depreciation sets in with "tearing oneself down," which is a form of self-hatred. "I made a mess out of my life. I'm no good to anybody. Everybody would be better off if I were dead." Some begin to obsessively dwell on past "sins," some small thing that gives them an excessive amount of guilt feelings. Feeling inadequate with very low self-esteem, the future looks "black" to the depressive. The ability to concentrate becomes poor and they cannot enjoy things they once enjoyed. There is also a loss of sexual interest and desire. In fact, all appetites are diminished.

As the depression deepens, delusions or false beliefs about the body may occur: "My insides have rotted away" or "my stomach has turned to stone." In psychotic depressions, auditory hallucinations may be present wherein the patient hears voices outside of himself that tell him he is doomed or going to be punished for some "evil" thing. Sometimes, the voices urge him to kill himself. The greatest danger, of course, is suicide. One must be aware of the "smiling depressive." When a very depressed person begins to smile and appears to be coming out of it, that is the time for more caution, because the individual may be smiling because he has decided to end his life as the only way out of his deep despair.

Sadness and grief are similar to fear in that the stimulus for these emotions is external and consciously recognized. Sadness is a normal feeling experienced when a son leaves for the armed services, a wallet is lost, one is fired from his job or we hear of some tragedy. Grief is experienced when a loved one or relative passes away. The degree of mourning is directly proportional to the degree of love and attachment to the deceased. Mourning can be dangerous to one's health. While mourning normally lasts up to one year, excessive and prolonged mourning leads to a seven-fold increase in morbidity. Dr. C.M. Parkes, a British psychiatrist, reported in a study of over-mourners and under-mourners that these individuals were more depressed, had an increased use of alcohol and tranquilizers, a tendency toward increased hospitalizations, a higher accident rate and higher death rate than normal mourners of similar age and status.

Some depressions occur secondarily to other external causes, such as the life-styles of the shut-in, chronic painful diseases and declining health. Others are a side effect of certain drugs that one might be taking. Some anti-hypertensive drugs such as reserpine, dopamine and clonidine, may cause depression. The chronic use of barbiturates, some minor tranquilizers, anti-cancer drugs, L-dopa (used in Parkinson's disease), digitalis, indomethacin, corticosteroids and alcohol can induce depression in some people. The answer is to check with your doctor about medications if a depression occurs for no obvious reason.

Physical disorders associated with depression include thyroid disturbances (hypothyroid), Cushing's disease, Addison's disease, diabetes, hypoglycemia (low blood sugar due to excessive insulin response to carbohydrate intake), pancreatic cancer, brain arteriosclerosis, hepatitis, viral pneumonia, influenza and infectious mononucleosis. These can be diagnosed by your doctor and when the underlying disorder is treated, the depression will lift, although anti-depressant drugs may also be utilized.

Current theories on the causes of depression are based on biochemical studies of brain metabolism and catecholamine imbalances at the synapses of brain cells. A synapse is the junction of linkages between brain cells. Catecholamines are substances such as tryptophane, nor-epinephrine, serotonin, dopamine, epinephrine, etc. There are hundreds of these amines present in the brain, and current anti-depressant drugs, such as tricyclics, MAO inhibitors, tetracyclics, amoxepine, trazadone, and other newer compounds, somehow increase the amount of these catecholamines at the synapses, thereby alleviating the depression. They are not without side-effects: commonly, dryness of the mouth, constipation, blurred vision and urinary retention. Some, tricyclics mainly, are risky in persons having glaucoma. A word about electro-stimulation therapy, this treatment is the safest and best for very severe depression, especially where the risk of suicide is present.

If you want to "beat the blues," make sure you get proper sleep. Sleep deprivation can cause lowered feelings and bleakness. Listening to cheerful, exciting music

28

often can lift someone out of the doldrums. Sometimes it is better to leave a blue person alone, rather than trying to cheer him up, and let the blues run their course. With others, talking it out with a trained counselor or psychiatrist is very helpful. Mild depressions can change with a change of scenery, buying a new hat, losing oneself in problems of other people, getting into some activity or reading the Bible. Remember, depression is treatable, so do not be afraid to seek professional help. It will be the best move you ever made.

6

THE FURY OF ANGER AND HATRED

HISTORIANS and theologians no doubt agree that the command to hate is as deeply imbedded in our nature as is the command to love. Human beings are capable of loving and hating themselves as well as others. Hatred is a blend of fear and anger, calling on the inborn survival mechanism for action. Students of hatred note that its physiological pattern is the same as that of fear and anger, namely the fight or flight response of the body's automatic nervous and hormonal systems. Since the birth of mankind, every society has had the formidable problem of controlling human hostility. Underlying this problem is the understanding between violence and communication, for violence is the final resort whenever a breakdown occurs in communication. Indeed, it may be the final communication in the murderous act. Anger, hate and hostility are destructive emotions, not only to those that possess them but to those to whom these emotions are directed.

The first recorded expression of hatred was the slaying of Abel by his brother Cain. Frustrated by God's admonition that acceptance depends on one's own good work, Cain lured his brother into the fields and slew him. Fraternal jealousy and hatred was also portrayed in Genesis 37 when Joseph's brothers conspired to kill him and later sold him into slavery to a passing caravan. David, whose music soothed King Saul's depressions, was the object of Saul's anger and murderous attempts. Saul later committed suicide when his hatred was turned within himself. Other notable figures who were consumed with hatred were Jonathan Swift, Richard Wagner, Alexander Pope, Adolf Hitler and John Wilkes Booth. From the "union" of anger and hatred are spawned the "offsprings" of prejudice, paranoia, rage, fury and violence.

Just what precisely is anger? Anger is a normal, natural emotion that has many forms, depending on the degree experienced: irritation, annoyance, displeasure, exasperation, seething resentment, discomfort, dismay, rage, frustration and fury. When we get angry, our autonomic nervous system gets flooded with impulses that affect our organs and bodily functions. Our heart rate accelerates, the respiration rate increases and blood pressure goes up. Our pupils dilate, skin hairs become erect and sweating occurs. Our voluntary muscles tighten and tremble. We get white-faced or purple with rage. In addition, our stomachs fill with acid and go into spasms.

Anger is really "outward anger," directed towards others; resentment is "inner anger," directed towards oneself. Hatred is anger with the aim of vengeance. Indignation is an intellectual justification for the feeling of anger, and irritability is a ready tendency towards anger. In spite of being a God-given emotion, many people attribute this feeling to possession by the devil and his cohorts, to evilness, immaturity or madness, i.e., "Are you nuts or somethin'?" While it is normal to get angry, how one deals with that anger is another matter. Controlling one's anger is vital, for we are the only species of primates who can hate, destroy and kill for months and years, and who can incite others to do likewise.

There are societies that can hate the "alien" in their midst as the Nazis against the Jews, whites vs. blacks, the religious persecutions, etc. Much humor that is sadistic is recognized as an outlet for generalized hate. Many acts of vandalism, rather than being done for "kicks," are actually due to frustration from anger caused by parental abuse, or lack of love in childhood. As soon as anyone becomes president of the United States, he automatically becomes the target of hundreds of paranoid patients in hospitals or out in the community.

We get angry as an emotional force to assist us in dealing with frustration, irritation and possible danger. It motivates one to seek reparation, satisfaction, to right a wrong or to protect oneself. Keeping these feelings inside habitually can lead to disease, but there is also a misguided notion that all anger must be expressed; that once it is released, one will no longer feel angry. This nonsense is found in fads and cults, as some encounter groups or "pop" counselors tell their clients to scream, swear or punch to "let it all out." This can be harmful and destructive.

Release does not lead to self-control nor does it solve the problem. Anger can only be moderated when it leads the person who is angry to do something constructive about whoever or whatever is causing the anger. For example, an angry wife should say to her husband: "What you are doing is making me have very angry feelings toward you. I care about you and I only want to have loving feelings toward you. If you give me the same consideration that you give other women, I won't feel this way." If something starts to irritate or frustrate you, or cause resentments, express it early before it builds up to rage, and try to do something about it. Change the situation that angers you. Sometimes this is impossible because others won't change their ways. Then we have to either accept it — realizing it is their problem. We can't let the actions of others get us down. If the action of others start to affect our physical or mental health, then it is our Christian duty to separate.

Dr. Rollo May, eminent psychologist, succinctly put it: "You cannot talk with someone as long as he is your enemy, and if you can talk with him, he ceases to be your enemy. When the bond between human beings is destroyed (when the possibilities for communication break down), aggression and violence will occur. Using violence to defeat violence will never work, whether it is done by police or administrators, or by young people themselves. Communication is the only way of understanding each other."

Of course, we have to decide whether our anger is justified. Some things are not really important, like "who ate the last cookie." Life is too short and much of our anger and resentments come from being too critical and expecting too much from others. "You can't make a silk purse out of a sow's ear," so we have to accept and love others in spite of their shortcomings. Charity, compassion and tolerance of the deficiencies of others diminishes the occurrence of anger. We should try to love as "God so loved the world." This kind of love suffers long, is patient and endures all things.

7

STRESS IS HOW YOU LOOK AT LIFE

WHEN I entered medical school after World War II, I learned about the human body structure by dissecting one in anatomy class, learning how it worked in physiology classes and what went wrong in disease in the study of pathology. As an intern four years later, I wished I could dissect the human mind, know more about how it worked and especially how to treat it. My experiences as an intern led me into the field of psychiatry. I saw a young girl slowly die of starvation (in spite of intravenous feedings) from a condition called anorexia nervosa. A young man in his prime bled to death from massive hemorrhages from ulcerative colitis, believed to be due to emotional stresses over a period of years. In general practice, I learned that over half the office patients had signs and symptoms for which no physical disease could be found, but were due to emotional stresses.

This is nothing new and many physicians over the centuries were aware of the effects of mind disturbances on the body. In the annals of Arabian medicine is recorded the experiences of a noted Persian physician, Rhazes, in the ninth century. His reputation for skills and good judgment brought him, as was the custom in those days, an appointment to look after royalty and the royal court. A young woman was brought to him who suffered from paralysis of both arms. After examining her, Rhazes asked her to stand in the presence of the assembled court. Without warning he removed her veil, causing her to blush deeply. Then he added to her indignity by suddenly raising her clothes over her head. The young lady instinctively lifted her arms to pull down her garments and thus was "cured."

While Webster's dictionary defines stress as "a strain, force or pressure exerted upon a body," stress is best understood as a set of physiological responses that a body makes to conditions which it finds disconcerting, disturbing or troublesome. A situation that is enjoyable to one person, such as taking an exam or public speaking, may be very stressful to another. Daily or frequent stresses over a period of time can cause "wear and tear" on the human body, leading to symptoms and disease. While America is the land of opportunity for life, liberty and the pursuit of happiness, unfortunately it is also a land of opportunity for stomach ulcers, hypertension, colitis and migraine headaches, especially for those in middle-management positions.

The pioneer studies of the action of stress on the body began intensively with Walter Cannon, who observed the effects of stress on emotions and the body, noting that fear, rage and pain produced changes in blood pressure, circulation, breathing rate and digestion. Cannon formulated his theory of stress arousing a person for "the emergency mobilization for fight or flight." The brilliant Canadian physician Dr. Hans Selye did stress research that led to his formulation of the "adaptation syndrome." He noted that stress produced an "alarm reaction" in the body as an inbred process of adaptation in which adrenal-cortical hormones were released. These hormones helped to reduce shock. However if the trauma was severe, great tissue changes occurred and even death could result. The sum and substance of his work was that shifts in the hormonal balances resulted from stress.

Regardless of class, everyone goes through life under some burden of anxiety and strain. Most people, as Thoreau said, "lead lives of quiet desperation." John Hunter, the eminent English surgeon, remarked: "My life is at the mercy of any rascal who can make me angry." It is a fact that shortly after he said this, he died in a fit of rage. Dis-equilibrium and disease occur with the combination of stress and certain personality types. The individual who is hard-driving, who is always engaged in some kind of purposeful activity and who faces considerable uncertainty is a prime candidate for the development of stress disorders.

During World War II, Commander Nardini described the reactions of Americans captured after the fall of Corregidor and Bataan. The U.S. prisoners of war were subjected to the gross stress reactions of capture, imprisonment and the cruelty of the Japanese. Deprived of name and rank, with no rights or justice, utter shock and depression set in. Many died in the first few months. Those who survived showed signs of mental regression. The survival instinct made them animal-like, quibbling over food; cheating and scheming to get another bowl of rice.

Stress can be real or it can be imagined, such as by a personality type that is too sensitive or too conscientious, perhaps jealous, envious or worrisome. Having negative attitudes induces some stress reactions. There is no doubt that shut-ins have real problems to face and deal with, but they also have anticipatory anxiety with a "tangled web" of doubts, uncertainty, insecurity and pressure that plays havoc with their health. Dealing with stress involves a change in outlook. Boredom, as well as understimulation, can be stressful to one's health also.

We do not hesitate to call a plumber if we cannot deal with leaky waterpipes by ourselves. So, if we have a nagging worry or difficulty, we should not hesitate to talk it over with a good friend, clergyman or physician. Talking it out brings some relief, a better perspective and some insight as to possible solutions. Sometimes our minds are so muddled that it is better to set the problem aside for awhile and escape into a good book, watch a movie or do something relaxing. When you feel more composed, come back to the problem. Jonathan Swift sagely suggested this piece of good advice to those who have a problem that they can't solve: "Think the problem not your own." In other words, if someone came to you with the same problem, what advice would you give them? Then, take that advice and do it.

Whatever stress makes you angry, just remember it's your stomach that's churning and nothing in this world is worth getting upset at. So, work off your anger in some housework and pray for the object of your anger. Don't make mountains out of molehills. Go easy with criticism and give in occasionally. Keep your life simple and take one thing at a time. Some people want to do too much or expect perfection from themselves and others. "Superman" is just a fantasy. Most importantly, take time out for hobbies and relaxation. I once asked a black woman, commenting on her sereneness and placidity, how she did it. She said: "When I work, I work. When I play, I play and when I sit, I sit." That is good advice for everyone.

8

THE MYSTERY OF MEMORY

IN 1948, at the Montreal Neurological Institute, the distinguished neurosurgeon, Dr. Wilder Penfield, performed brain surgery on an epileptic female under a local anesthetic. He wanted to avoid injuring the brain areas for sensory location and he touched a spot on the side of the exposed cortex, the outer layer of the brain, with a tiny, stimulating electrode. Immediately, the woman said to the doctor: "I hear music." When the electrode was removed, the music stopped. Each time he touched it she heard the same song, not an imaginary tune but a full orchestration as if she were reliving some past experience. More fascinating was the fact that each time the stimulation occurred the music began from the beginning.

Dr. Penfield commented that it was as if the memory areas of the brain were like magnetic recording tape, capable of being played over and over. Indeed, from the moment that we enter into the world until we give our last gasp, every waking experience is recorded permanently within our brain. One of the most basic properties of the mind, memory is vital to recall the past and necessary to intelligence. As Cicero stated: "Memory is the treasure and guardian of all things." Many things have been said about memory, but none more lovely than the Scottish dramatist James Barrie, who said: "God gave us our memories so that we might have roses in December."

While memory is a mental process which includes the taking and retaining of information and its subsequent recall and recognition, this process is not infallible and we often have trouble with our memory. It may also have to do with the value we place on things. I may not remember where I set my glasses down, but I never forgot that Jack owes me five bucks. Far too often, we wish we could remember certain things and there is a great deal we wish we could forget. Children are able to take in, and retain, but they are not able to assimilate and coordinate their memories for their benefit and use.

It has been estimated that some 15 trillion bits of information are received, sorted and perhaps stored in the average human brain in a lifetime of 70 years. While intelligent people have good memories, they are not always able to use them well. In the memory process, any experience makes an impression and a record of this impression is retained. This is followed later by a reentry into one's conscious mind of this record. Records are made even of impressions or sensations which did not enter awareness and they can be remembered clearly under hypnosis.

In fact, it is impossible to prove that anything once learned is ever completely forgotten. Every experience is "filed" in the memory areas of the brain under "headings" of "important," "pleasant," "dangerous," etc., and associated with some kind of emotion appropriate to it. Material that has meaning is learned much more quickly than dull data and also is forgotten more slowly. The bright student who is a fast learner does not necessarily do better on examinations because of a superior memory, but because he or she has learned the subject more efficiently. If a slow student spends more time on learning material, he or she will retain it as well as the fast learner. Most "memory improvement" courses concentrate on accomplishing better learning by making new material more meaningful.

Defects of memory are of three types: defective recording, defective retention and defective reproduction. Defective recording may be due to poor concentration, visual or hearing problems, nervousness, a "racing mind," fatigue or where brain function is impaired by alcohol or drugs. Defective retention is always due to brain injuries or disease and brain degeneration. Concussion, skull factures and hardening of the arteries to the brain are most common. So damage to brain cells or poor circulation to them impairs memory retention. Everyone throughout life has problems with "remembering," or reproduction, due to a variety of causes.

Children frequently forget to wash their hands, come home on time or pick up their toys. Teenagers forget to cut the grass, take out the garbage or also to be home on time. Adults forget names, phone numbers, to pay bills or to buy some item while grocery shopping. They and we take these things for granted: they probably didn't pay attention or they had other things on their minds. However, if one is over 50 and forgets, the fear that they are getting senile pops into their head. Often, the attitude of others around them conveys that notion. "It must be old age." Forgetfulness in the elderly is often caused by anxiety, fatigue, lack of concentration and sometimes the sedating or side effects of certain medications they are taking.

In senility, memory impairment begins with recent memory forgetfulness and progresses backward in time so that a person may think it is 1952 and the children are all in school, etc. The last parts of memory to be acquired are the first to go. Amnesia, or loss of memory, occurs in brain damage like concussion or contusion and in psychological shocks as hysterical amnesia. This latter is a defense against the coming into consciousness of an event which is unbearably painful. Sometimes we "forget" to do something because of a conflict between a conscious or unconscious need and the proposed act.

Our emotional attitudes and needs may affect our memory. For example, if two people witness the same event, each will honestly remember those details that are in harmony with his needs and will tend to forget those that are not. The more often that information is used, the longer it is remembered. The human brain has a right and left hemisphere that control opposite sides of the body, with one side being dominant. If you are right-handed, the left side of your brain is dominant and the right side is for left-handers. The famous French physician Louis Pasteur suffered a brain hemorrhage that damaged half his brain, but, because the dominant half was undamaged, he wasn't kept from doing some of his best work.

How memory takes place in the brain itself has been the object of intensive studies. It is generally believed that each experience is registered in brain cells by changes in nucleoproteins and that RNA, or ribonucleic acid, may have a role in the memory process. Still, memory can be improved by concentration, the use of association and practice. The use of associated sounds is often employed, such as if Mr. Kelly has a protruding abdomen (belly), it will remind you of Kelly. Make an effort to remember by concentrating and write down anything important you want to remember and repeatedly say it aloud. Active memorizing is better than silent reading. If one goes to sleep after learning, one retains it in his memory better than if he continued his daily activities.

Good nutrition and good circulation help brain function and memory. If you have any problem in these areas, consult your physician. There are drugs available today, such as Hydergine, which aids blood circulation in the brain. There are several nutrients, obtainable at health food stores, which promote mental alertness. These are: ribonucleic acid (about 300 mgs daily), choline (900 mgs daily), phenylalanine (150 mgs daily) and L-Glutamine (50 mgs daily). Lastly, do not overtire yourself, and lead a balanced life. As Alexander Smith said: "A man's real possession is his memory. In nothing else is he rich, in nothing else is he poor."

9

DEATH: THE FINAL AWAKENING

IF there is a universal fear that has existed since the beginning of mankind, it would be thanatophobia, or the fear of death. In the life cycle of every human being, death is the final stage and the inevitable outcome of every life story. For most individuals, death is something somber, terrifying, fearsome and awesome. The contemplation of death provokes anxiety and dread. This phenomenon of varied reactions and attitudes has led to a new scientific discipline called thanatology or the study of dying and death. If we are to dispel or modify the fear of death, we must understand it, its causes and how to accept it. Sir Walter Scott, poet and novelist, wrote: "Is death the last sleep? No, it is the final awakening."

Much of the basis of these fear attitudes toward death lies in the nature of present-day society, a society that is based on a value system of material goods, power, prestige, worship of the self and the pursuit of pleasure, not to mention the avoidance of pain, as witness our abuse of drugs and alcohol. We also are driven by an instinct of self-preservation and survival. Moreover, we live in a society that glorifies youth and displays irreverence for the aged who are shunned and who fare worse than pet animals. There is no society for the prevention of cruelty to the elderly.

It is indeed a sad commentary on the times that 75% of those who die today, die in institutions like hospitals, hospices or nursing homes. In the "olden" days, one died at home with his family around the bedside. While they were dying, their loved ones were about them and they were not alone. They died with dignity and the love, compassion and comfort of their loved ones. They were not separated from them in their last hours.

Today, the dying are often left alone in cold, sterile hospital rooms, separated from spouses and children, delicately avoided by nurses and doctors (for the fear of death affects even those who minister to the dying), to suffer the mental and physical anguish alone. As Christ said: "So, could you not watch with me one hour?" (Mt. 26:40)." Many doctors and nurses do not realize that, even though there is nothing more that they can do medically when a person is dying, this is when the patient needs them the most. The dying need to talk about their feelings and they need understanding, comfort and not to feel abandoned. They have a fear of the unknown, a fear of loneliness, a fear of separation from their family, a fear of loss of self-control and a fear of pain.

The fear of death is not only based on a fear of the unknown but on separation anxiety. Around the age of four or five a child usually becomes aware of death as being the end of life. A child fears the death of his mother or father as well as a separation anxiety. It is a fear of isolation without a protecting mother. Children don't really understand death, and the belief of life after death, when they will be with their parents, seems to sustain them. In adult life, concerns over death transcend the self, and others are willing to die to save their children or fellow-men. Sigmund Freud stated that to endure life remains, when all is said, the first duty of all human beings. Illusion can have no value if it makes this more difficult for us. If you would endure life, be prepared for death. Death is only tempting when life becomes burdensome, when life becomes "hell on earth."

In his play, "Hamlet," Shakespeare says: "To be, or not to be, that is the question . . . 'tis a consummation devoutly to be wished, to die, to sleep; but that dread of something after death, makes us rather bear those ills we have." Strangely, but understandably, it is those who have never been able to live, either because others have restricted them or because of personality problems, who seem to fear death the most and cling to life as their most precious possession. What we can't accept is that death is as natural an event as birth.

Well-adjusted personalities, especially those with a deep faith in God and His teachings, generally have an acceptance of dying and death. Those with emotional or nervous personalities have a great deal of apprehension in dying. Dying patients cope with the stress of dying in the same way they have previously coped with other life stresses. And then there are others who are apathetic and show no feelings about it, while some look forward to death with anticipation.

When a person is told he or she is going to die, certain reactions seem to occur. At first, there is shock and disbelief. "It can't be true. I want a second opinion." There may even be denial and isolation. Then may follow anger and resentment: "Why me? After all I've done in life. It isn't right or fair. I've got so much to live for and do." Some get angry at God and become bitter: "What did I do to deserve this?" After rage and resentment comes depression, with a sense of loss and grief. Finally, comes acceptance and detachment, a wish to be left alone. In the last dying moments, there is a serene, peaceful state

47

that comes over the individual. Patients who have been clinically dead and, through vigorous resuscitation have come back to life, have reported a beautiful, peaceful feeling and some resented being brought back because it was such a joyous experience.

Generally, patients who are dying should be told the truth and assisted in the acceptance of this final act of life. In dealing with the dying, there is no set plan, only to be caring, honest and understanding. Listen and respond to whatever they wish to talk about. They don't want advice or answers, only understanding. The idea is to share their feelings and the only solution is acceptance. We want to comfort them physically (hold their hand), emotionally (I care and I share) and spiritually (God is with you).

Bertrand Russell thought of death as the concluding episode of one's life plan: "An individual's human existence should be like a river . . . small at first, narrowly contained within its banks, and rushing passionately past boulders, and over waterfalls. Gradually, the river grows wider, the banks recede, the waters flow more quietly and, in the end, without any visible break, they become merged in the sea, and painlessly lose their individual being."

Death is something not to be denied nor feared. Why and how we die when we do, only God knows and understands. As Cardinal Newman said in his Meditation Prayer: "I know not what purpose I have in life, but He knows." Life is temporary, so be moderate in all things, have a love in your heart for Him and when the time comes, accept it as going through the last door in life and awakening in the presence of the Lord.

10

POSITIVE ATTITUDES: KEYS TO ACHIEVEMENT

WATCHING people travel down the "road of life," it soon becomes apparent that far too many individuals fail to achieve their potential or to develop their God-given talents — and for many reasons. When it comes to achievement, most people get very few "miles to the gallon" of living. We all have a drive to better ourselves that is part of our nature. We want to excel and be "good" at something. Sophocles, the Athenian poet, believed: "As long as you are living, you have purpose." Yet, in spite of their accomplishments, many find themselves with feelings of disillusionment and disappointment, dwelling on the gap between what they wished to have become and what they have become, with regrets.

What prevents most people from achievement are the shackles of negative attitudes, lack of self-confidence, lack of effort, fear of failure and procrastination, a lack of stick-to-it-iveness. Sometimes, it is our attitude that is at fault. Many individuals complain that their job is too dull or boring. The fact of the matter is that every job or profession has it's boring aspects. It is true that one job may be more interesting than another, but not nearly as true as that one mind is more interested than another. Every job has it's own dignity.

It is never too late in life to do anything within reason. History shows us that we can learn at any age and that we can be successful at any age in mental activities. A positive attitude is necessary, not giving in to feelings of inadequacy, feelings of failure or feelings that "I'll never be able to do it." As they say Recovery, a self-help group: "Feelings are not facts." For those afraid of trying and failing, Abraham Lincoln put it thusly: "I am not bound to succeed, but I am bound to live up to what light I have."

Someone once asked a wise man how he came to acquire his wisdom. He replied: "Because I have good judgment, and that came from having had bad judgment." In other words, everyone makes mistakes and everyone has experienced many failures. We learn from our mistakes. "A mistake is only a friendly invitation to keep trying." What hinders many persons is a low self-image, lack of self-esteem and a fear of trying new things. Human beings, like things in nature, suffer from inertia. Decision is of little account unless it is followed by action. Too many individuals desire achievement or success without effort or planning, and that can never be.

Optimism and pessimism are opposite attitudes present in everyone to some degree and more so in others. These attitudes affect our outlook, our progress toward our goals and our relationships with others. A positive attitude comes from having faith in God and in ourselves, with confidence that persistence will eventually pay off. Some people seem to get more than their share of "bumps and bruises" in life, but do not waste time feeling sorry for themselves. They pack it away, smile and keep trying to do their best. Robert Louis Stevenson, who wrote *Treasure Island* and other great stories, was a shut-in who was desperately ill most of his adult life and had to do his writing in bed. He left a priceless legacy of exciting and inspiring literature.

The Old Testament's "As a man thinketh in his heart, so is he" and Buddha's "All that we are is the result of what we have thought" led writer James Allen to say: "Faith bestows that sublime courage that rises superior to troubles and disappointments in life, that acknowledges no defeat except as a step to victory; that is strong to endure, patient to wait, and energetic to struggle. Where faith is, there is courage, there is fortitude, there is steadfastness and strength." We can develop a positive attitude by changing the way we look at things and endeavoring to be really what we wish to appear. Motive is the force behind the thought of a desirable goal. Every person has the ability to change his character through conscious effort.

The difficulty lies in the fact that there are some who do not want to give up their childish ways and habits. They fear any change and worry excessively about their abilities. According to Dr. Thomas S. Kepler, only 8% of our worries are real, 40% will never happen, 12% are over old decisions, 30% are over people's criticisms of us and 10% are about our health. Who knows, or pays heed, to the timeless truth of Marcus Aurelius, the Roman emperor and philosopher, who said: "Very little is needed to make a happy life; it is all within ourselves, in our way of thinking."

An Indian swami once drew a two-foot line on a blackboard, turned toward his students and said: Which of you can make this line smaller without touching it?" After much pondering and deliberation, no one knew how to accomplish this. The swami then said: "I will now show you how." He turned and drew a three-foot line above it. Now the line was smaller — by comparison. Inferiority is a state of mind that is often induced by comparison with others in any area of attribute. Disraeli wrote: "Life is too short to be little." Let us accept ourselves as we are and use our talents, whatever they may be, in helping others.

A handicap may be an advantage in bowling or golf but it is considered a disadvantage if it impedes our lifestyle and adjustment, such as with emphysema or severe heart disease. Still, there have been many persons with handicaps that have persevered and turned them into advantages of sorts. Byron, in spite of his clubfeet, learned to dance perfectly. Stuttering Demosthenes became a great orator and Renoir, the painter, was so crippled by rheumatism that his brushes had to be strapped to his fingers. He kept painting until his last day of life.

Whatever your disability, accept it as a challenge and as part of your purpose in God's plan for you. Treasure and enjoy your friendships. Be loving and warm to children when in their presence. Look for the best in everyone and try to bring out the best in them. Avoid whining and self-pity, for they do no good. Your positive attitudes are contagious and bring success.

11

LOVE, GOD-STYLE

THE most powerful force in this world is the power of love. While we all possess the capacity to love, few have the ability to love, let alone a true understanding of the nature of love. While it has been called the folly of a wise man and the only wisdom of a fool, love cannot be measured nor examined scientifically. Poets, philosophers, psychologists and priests, doctors, lawyers and "Indian chiefs" have all expounded on the character of love, but it still seems to be a sublime mystery. The essence of love may never be quite completely understood, but there are aspects of it that are known.

You would not suspect this by looking at the world around us today. In a society that has never been as educated, surrounded by technology at its finest, we have more problems and misery than we can handle. Our educational institutions have turned out a lot of people with million-dollar brains and ten-cent hearts. Some of these people know how to take your car apart, but they wouldn't stop to help you push it. The substance of education has been to focus on facts and figures, but seems to have ignored feelings. Most of the books on love today concentrate on a part of the anatomy that has no connection to the heart and what life is really all about, much less love.

Since nature and temperament are inherited, it follows that some people are "born lovers," that is, they have a generous and loving disposition. Others seem to have inherited a "refrigerated disposition that simply can't defrost." Since it is true that you "can't make a silk purse out of a sow's ear," it is frustrating to watch some spouses continually trying to change their mates into a romantic figure instead of accepting them as they are and appreciating their efforts. Being openly loving is very difficult for some individuals who lack that warmth and spontaneity. The ability to love varies with each person, depending on one's hereditary disposition, upbringing and life experiences. Nevertheless, we can all strengthen our "love muscle" by understanding and making a habit out of loving.

The emotion of love has been variously described as a strong feeling of attachment or deep affection, as charity, as fondness and as passion. Love appears to be a rainbow of desires, each blending in a spectrum of dynamic strivings that draws us to those we love. Many feelings are falsely called "love," but true love asks nothing in return and is a power for goodness. Sexual desire, on the other hand, is not love but an instinct that exists for the preservation of the species, not with the improvement of it. While we can desire without loving, we cannot love without desiring. Desiring is a physical experience and dies with fulfillment, whereas love is never completely satisfied and lasts forever.

Undoubtedly, there are more jokes made about love and marriage than any other category. Supposedly based on love, marriage is generally portrayed as disguised or open aggression and hostility. One often wonders what makes "loved ones" behave so irrationally at times. Helen Rowland, a humorous author and columnist, commented years ago: "Love is the quest; marriage, the conquest; and divorce, the inquest. Before marriage, a man will lie awake all night thinking about something you said; after marriage, he'll fall asleep before you finish saying it." Marriages usually fail because people fail as individuals. Failure starts when a spouse begins to put one's mate out of one's heart. This kind of love is immature, self-centered and demanding.

To understand the nature of love, one has to simply study the perfect Model of love, Jesus Christ. He lived and taught compassion, forgiveness, giving of oneself and faith in God. The Bible contains numerous examples wherein Jesus emphasized the importance of forgiveness, an element lacking in most marriages today. He gave comfort and reassurance to those in pain and suffering. He rejected no one and He frequently spoke of the need for understanding and acceptance. He pointed out false values and goals, and His roadmap for our journey through life was based simply on the Commandments with the emphasis on: "Love the Lord your God with all your heart, and with all your soul and with all your mind. . . . You shall love your neighbor as yourself" (Matthew 22:37-39).

Just as with children, all adults need the three A's: affection, acceptance and approval. Giving, as part of the essence of love, means attending to the needs of those around us every day, in any way that we can. We tend to get so wrapped up in our own concerns that we often are unmindful of the concerns of others. Look at them, be alert to their moods and listen to what they are saying. Being compassionate is not a matter of giving advice as much as just showing that we care and understand. Be positive and patient. Encourage, comfort and give hope. If you can help in any way, do so.

One of the problems in human relationships is that we tend to expect too much from other people and frequently we get hurt and disappointed. Sir William Osler, who was professor of medicine at the John Hopkins University School of Medicine years ago, wrote a book for physicians entitled *Aequanimitas*. It was a book designed to help doctors get peace of mind, to deal with the stresses of patient care. His first principle was: "Expect little from those around you." If we expect people around us to be kind, thoughtful, considerate, appreciative, etc., we will most often be disappointed. Because most people have their own character defects and moods, their own problems, they cannot behave any way we would like them to behave. Besides, we are only accountable for our own actions, not theirs.

Forgiving is part of true love, as well as forgetting. The latter part is difficult because we often tend to dwell on our hurts and throw it up to the offending party at a later time. Mature love does not expect perfection in others, but implies a willingness to sacrifice oneself for the betterment of others. Face each day as it comes and every morning spend a few moments in contemplation. Like athletes who "psych" themselves up for their event, we should also "psych" ourselves into a positive, loving attitude and determine to imitate the love of Christ in our daily lives.

12

BRIGHTEN YOUR DAY WITH LAUGHTER

CHAPTER three, verses 1-4, in the Book of Ecclesiastes contains the admonitions of Solomon that, "For everything there is a season, and a time for every matter under heaven. . . ." He tells us that there is a time to weep, and a time to laugh. As for myself, I have always had the belief that one cannot survive the pitfalls and crises of life without a sense of humor. It has always sustained me in dire moments and helped to ease my tensions. Human beings are the only animals that have the power to laugh. Nietzsche, the German philosopher, commented that man suffers so much he had to invent laughter. There is no doubt that laughter is essential to stability and good health. William Hazlitt wrote that man laughs and weeps because he is the only creature that is struck with the difference between what things are and what they ought to be.

Laughter is a form of communication, and laughing releases repressed energy that keeps hostility under wraps. It is not only used to express released tensions of aggression or anxiety, but also to express joy and elation, amusement and triumph, embarrassment and scorn, relief and derision. Anxieties are often mastered with humor, as "laughing at your troubles." One observation is that many fine speakers begin their talks with a few humorous stories or jokes to relax their audiences.

A joke or witticism starts with an insulting or shocking thought. This must be repressed, since our conscience forbids it. In our unconscious mind, this thought gets "dressed up" and disguised. Later, it comes out in our conscious mind as a joke or funny saying. Laughter then occurs when the repressing energy is freed or released from keeping this forbidden thought under repression. This reaction of the listener will show if this process has been successful, that is, he *must* laugh. If the listener doesn't laugh, the teller will feel badly, ashamed or perhaps even guilty.

Some jokes are novel, such as: "Why did Adam and Eve have an ideal marriage? Because he didn't have to listen to her stories about all the other men she could have married, and she didn't have to listen to his about his mother's cooking." Cutting hostility is exemplified in this story of a meeting between George Bernard Shaw and the beautiful dancer, Isadora Duncan. She gushingly said: "Mr. Shaw! With your brains and my beauty, we should have a baby together." He acidly replied: "With my luck, it would have my looks and your brains!"

Life often is tough enough and we have to laugh at ourselves and others rather than to indulge in self-pity and become depressed. Like the old man who said: "Last night I unscrewed my wooden leg and put it in the drawer. I put my false teeth, glass eye and toupee in the drawer. Then, I didn't know whether to go to bed or get in the drawer." As Ma Barnes puts it: "Life's really good, important things are the simple things, I've found. A little ray of sunshine . . . a penny on the ground. A true friend, and a kindness, a life that's free from sin, a little smile from those you love . . . a little nip of gin."

Laughing is a good way to release tension and it puts one at ease, especially in group situations. It reduces muscle tension, relaxes tissues, increases oxygenation and stimulates various glands as well as the central nervous system. It actually stimulates the heart, increasing the heart rate and the force of the heartbeat. Paradoxically, it increases the blood pressure if it is low and lowers the pressure if it is high.

Now, here is what happens physically when you laugh: You take in deep breath inspirations and expel them in short, interrupted bursts. The muscles of the throat, neck and chest are agitated and the diaphragm is violently shaken in clonic spasms. As your eyelids are elevated, your eyes will brighten and may water as the tear glands are compressed by the distended cheeks and muscles about the eyelids. Your lower jaw vibrates and your arteries dilate. Body temperature rises and hormone glands are stimulated. In case you are wondering about all this analysis, just remember that the definition of a psychiatrist is a guy who goes to a burlesque show and looks at the audience.

The Bible truly is the source of all wisdom and, paraphrased, Proverbs (18:14) says: "A cheerful heart does good like medicine, but a broken spirit makes one sick." The well-known Canadian scientist, Dr. Hans Selye, pioneered the studies of negative emotions on body health. His work showed how feelings of frustration, anger, rage, envy, anxiety and depression affected body health. As stress factors, these negative emotions lead to adrenal exhaustion and ill health.

It was these findings that led Norman Cousins, a prominent editor who came down with a serious disease, to believe that positive emotions would promote better health and healing. In his fine book *Anatomy Of An Illness As Perceived By The Patient* he describes how

59

he got better by a daily program of watching humorous movies and reading books that made him laugh. He and his doctor noted that daily laughter had a beneficial effect on his condition, from a pathophysiological point of view. Laughter was indeed "good medicine."

Our late beloved President John F. Kennedy once stated: "There are three things in life that are real: God, human folly and laughter. The first two are beyond our comprehension. Let us make most of the last." Having a sense of humor helps us to keep things in their proper perspective. Part of our daily activities should include some aspect of humor designed to tickle our funny bone. One way for the shut-in to do this is in reading good, humorous books that one can obtain from a library. There is a wealth of good humor in books by authors such as Robert Benchley, James Thurber, Stephen Leacock, Ogden Nash, Neil Simon and many others. There are many fine joke books by contemporary comedians. Television often has movies and sit-coms that provide many a laugh and release from daily tensions. Consult your local library for assistance and service. As Oscar Wilde said: "Laughter is not a bad beginning for a friendship, and it is the best ending for one."

13

IN MY SOLITUDE

THE records of history are the story of man as a social being and of the building of civilizations, but history has not really recorded his inner life of aloneness. Aloneness is the condition of being alone, separated from others and one's world. For many, it is a state of abandonment and depression, but to some clergy, philosophers and poets, aloneness brings serenity and an opportunity for contemplation. To adventurers, it is a solitude that yields a joy in dominating a domain they alone have mastered. Yet, to others, aloneness may bring boredom or madness. It follows therefore that one's character strengths or weaknesses determine whether aloneness is looked upon as loneliness or solitude.

Most of the world's greatest religious figures prepared for their life's role through meditation conducted in solitude. Jesus Christ spent 40 days in the desert, fasting and praying. The prophet Mohammed retired twice to the wilderness. Buddha left a life of luxury and sought enlightenment in seven years of austerity. Later, he sat under a bo tree and vowed not to stir until he had solved the riddle of life. In the third century, St. Anthony founded a community of solitude in the Arabian desert, attracting other hermits, and they devoted themselves to prayer and penance while living together in an abandoned fort.

Some writers have found complete solitude as a necessary condition for creative work. Goethe thought that "talent is best nurtured in solitude," and Robert Louis Stevenson considered solitude a pure pleasure. For Anne Morrow Lindbergh, solitude was the serenity found in walking alone on an island beach. "How wonderful are islands! Islands in space, like this one I have come to, ringed about by miles of water, linked by no bridges, no cables, no telephones. An island from the world and the world's life. Islands in time, like this short vacation of mine. The past and the future are cut off; only the present remains. People, too, become like islands in such an atmosphere, self-contained, whole and serene; respecting other people's solitude, not intruding on their shores, standing back in reverence before the miracle of another individual."

Our attitudes toward the world around us and our relationships are in part dependent on our inherited temperaments and our personalities. While some people are alone by choice, many find themselves alone often because of difficult and unhealthy personalities. The paranoid or suspicious type alienates others by his angry, "feel-cheated," "I-don't-trust-anybody-because-they're-out-to-getcha" attitude. The narcissistic or egotistical type is avoided by others because all he ever talks about is himself, his needs and his problems. Some people are incessant, boring talkers. It appears as if their tongues were born and the rest of them grew on. We generally avoid anyone who gives us pain, boredom, anger and anx_iety.

Shut-ins, by the nature of their existence and their

problems, live in their "island" of aloneness and should learn how to utilize solitude to enrich their lives. Ralph Emerson said: "A man's defects are made useful to him and he draws strength from his weaknesses and, like the wounded oyster, mends his shell with pearl." There are many activities for shut-ins that are strengthening to the soul, rewarding to the mind, entertaining, fulfilling and useful.

Meditation can add a new dimension to one's spiritual life. Set aside 20 minutes daily in a quiet spot and select any beneficial and inspiring verse of Scripture to read. Read it over a few times and then dwell on what you have read. Think of how this might apply to your life. Praise God for His Truths and blessings. Then, spend some time in prayer, because God always listens and is understanding. If you don't have a Bible, call your pastor or any religious group that would be happy to supply you with one.

Get interested in other people and reach out to make friends. If you have children or grandchildren, call or write to them regularly. Sharing of ourselves with others may only require a simple smile or gesture. Use your wits and think up little kindnesses you can do for others. George Bernard Shaw insisted that "we have no more right to consume happiness without producing it than to consume wealth without producing it." When you think of it, the only way to have a friend is to be one.

Another activity we can do in solitude is reading. Books are friends, a way of escaping from the tedium of life, a promoter of thoughts and ideas. A good book gives you the feeling that you are being inspired, informed, helped or entertained. The selection of books is highly personal, but I would recommend the classics, and two good books to start with are Wells' *Outline of History* and Will Durant's *Story of Philosophy*. Life is one long process of learning, and as we climb "successive hills" we ask what lies beyond. If your eyesight is extremely poor, ask your librarian for cassettes.

If you have no hobbies, you can find one that might appeal to you, such as knitting, crocheting, woodworking, painting, ceramics, collecting or doing crossword puzzles. Some people enjoy entering contests. Music is another form of entertainment, whether one plays an instrument or listens to the radio. If you have a Christian station on your radio band, it can be a great source of comfort and education.

For those who are able, taking part in church social work, such as mending clothes for the poor, or any kind of assistance that they might need, is an act of charity. There is always something that you can do, but it is up to you to do it. Remember what Dr. Seth Helsper said: "I have noticed that people who use rocking chairs seldom suffer from constipation." Don't let your enthusiasm batteries run down, but do interesting things you never even thought of doing before. Solitude can be creative and adventuresome.

14

THE FORGOTTEN ART OF RELAXATION

ONE morning at sunrise years ago in New York City, I got up and went to the window of my hotel room to look out at Manhattan. The sight I saw immediately conjured up a vision of a giant ant farm. Hundreds of people were pouring out of those holes in the ground called subway stations. They scurried along the sidewalks, dodging and jostling each other. The streets were jammed with cars and frenzied drivers vented their spleen on raucous horns as garment-workers pushed their swaying dollies through the maze of traffic. The only stationary figure was an elderly wino sleeping in a doorway.

Look at the world today and you will see members of the "rat race" rushing on a never-ending treadmill of activities, the ravages of our modern civilization. We live in an age of stressful and harried existence. Caught in the web of tension and frustration, modern man struggles and ends up coping in a most unhealthy fashion by abusing eating, drinking, drugs, sex, work and recreation.

Most people just do not know how to relax or enjoy leisure time.

In 1800, the average worker toiled 14 hours a day, six days a week. Today, the working person is facing the possibility of a 32-hour, four-day week. This has caused the eminent psychiatrist Dr. Karl Menninger to state: "Our nation would be in peril if suddenly every man in the U.S. had to work only half his present hours. He would not know what to do. Some would play, but the rest would be fighting, drinking and killing each other off." Because so many people do not know how to relax and are continuously tense, the "self-help" bookshelves in stores are crammed with a variety of manuals designed to guide one to relaxation, serenity and peace of mind. These include self-hypnosis, behavior modification, yoga, mind control, etc.

Leisure has been defined as "time at one's command," and relaxation is "a lessening or loosening of tension from effort or work." The command in the Army was, "At ease, men!" A great deal can be learned about one's personality by one's use of free time. Primitive men used their leisure time, with dances and ceremonials, as a reflection of concern over the basic questions of life and death. The Greeks used leisure for activities such as drama, athletics, oratory, poetry and music. Evidently, the stress was on intellectual pursuits, for the word "school" comes from "skhole," the Greek word for leisure.

The Romans worked from dawn until noon, and then spent the afternoon and evening watching sports and attending orgies of various sorts. Today we watch sports and various orgies on television. The guilds in the Middle Ages invented the three eights: eight hours of work, eight hours of leisure and eight hours of sleep. Then the Puritans came along with the dictum of "all work and no play," even proscribing Christmas. Now we spend over 60 billion dollars yearly for recreational goods and services. Instead of being restful and fulfilling, it has become a nightmare of joining health spas and clubs, agonizing jogging, aerobic dancing, drinking parties, guided tours and agitated golfing — leading to hypertension, coronaries, ulcers and an early grave.

The modern housewife is a combination cook, housekeeper, mother, lover, chauffeur, nurse, den mother, charity fund collector, handyman and you-name-it. She drinks to relax and finds herself on the road to alcoholism. Most people do not live wisely nor do they know how to relax. Instead of finding out what they alone are interested in, they conform to what others do and to what is socially the "rage." Some wit once defined relaxation as "loungitude and lassitude," but the truth is we can't even loaf without feeling guilty.

The Book of Sirach contains a little gem on sensible living that says: "The wisdom of a learned man cometh by opportunity of leisure; and he that hath little business shall become wise." Happiness is enjoying what you get and not what you want. Just sitting and thinking positive thoughts can be relaxing. One does not necessarily have to accomplish anything. Exercise and sports should simply be considered as a way of keeping healthy, not just for competition.

The aim of leisure should be for creativity and the development of mind and spirit. It is a pride in doing something good and pleasant that isn't too taxing or a strain. I like to relax by sitting in a quiet church. Some relax on a couch listening to their favorite music. In order to relax, one has to empty one's mind of all worldly matters and problems. Put them in God's hands for the time being and just relax.

Here is a technique for learning how to relax your body and your mind. Practice it once or twice daily. (1) Sit quietly in a comfortable position in an easy chair. (2) Close your eyes. (3) Deeply relax all your muscles. Think of your arms and legs as being made of concrete and you can't move them. Keep them relaxed by thinking over and over that they are warm, relaxed, that this is a pleasant feeling. (4) Breathe through your nose. Become aware of your breathing. As you breathe out, say the word "peace" to yourself silently. For example, breathe in . . . out, "peace", in . . . out, "peace", etc. (5) Continue for 20 minutes. You may open your eyes to check the time, but do not use an alarm. When you finish, sit quietly for several minutes with closed eyes and later with opened eyes. During this time, think of something or someone pleasant. (6) Do not worry about whether you are successful in achieving a deep level of relaxation.

Maintain a passive attitude and permit relaxation to occur at its own pace. When distracting thoughts occur, ignore them and continue repeating "peace." With practice, the response should come with little effort. Try to practice twice daily, but not within two hours after any meal, since the digestive processes seem to interfere with the production of anticipated changes. Remember, it took years of practice to get to be an accomplished worrier, so it takes practice and repeated effort to replace this habit with one of being relaxed.

15

BE A FRIEND, HAVE A FRIEND

A FAITHFUL friend is a sturdy shelter, and he that hath found one has found a treasure. There is nothing so precious as a faithful friend, and no scales can measure his excellence (Sirach 6:14-15).

The classic example of friendship of the highest order is described as having taken place in the fourth century B.C. in Syracuse, then in southeastern Sicily, with the tale of Damon and Pythias. A tyrant, Dionysius I, sentenced Pythias to die for plotting against him. Damon, Pythias' friend, offered himself as a hostage so that Pythias could take one last journey home to straighten his affairs. When Pythias was delayed, Damon was condemned to die in his place. At the last moment, Pythias hurried back and surrendered in order to save his friend. The mutual loyalty so moved the king that he spared them both and asked permission to join as a member in their pact.

Friendship is a human, intimate relationship that is

based on choice and the love of one person for another. It is based on a range of emotions from the deepest love, as characterized by complete sacrifice, to the shallow relationship of "fair-weather" friends. Just as with love, it can be motivated by personal gain and selfish interests or by mutual pursuit of the highest good. David Hume cynically remarked that "the difficulty is not so great to die for a friend, as to find a friend worth dying for." Most people want to be friendly and loving but find themselves hampered by personal likes and dislikes. Disliking people requires a reason, while loving does not. As Henry Ward Beecher said: "Every man should have a fair-sized cemetery in which to bury the faults of his friends."

Human beings by their very nature are not "islands unto themselves," but need friendship which is necessary to the enjoyment of life, for friendship is the art of "loving thy neighbor as thyself." We also need friends for love, inspiration, approval, comfort, criticism and entertainment. An environment of friends is beyond price. Making friends, however, is about nine-tenths doing and one-tenth talking. Love, like money, must be invested wisely in order to return dividends. If it is "hoarded," it diminishes in value.

The self-centered person is an unpleasant personality who is a slave to himself and so cannot be a friend to others. The fault-finding person with his excessive criticism creates tension and builds unhappiness. He may criticize the state of the world around him without doing anything effectively to better it. Envious people are foolish people because they cannot enjoy anything pleasant without souring it by thinking that so-and-so had a better experience. Fear is also another powerful enemy of friendship. It makes us avoid people because of imaginary feelings of being possibly hurt or rejected.

In order to develop strong friendships, there are three personality factors that we must have or develop. Firstly, we must love ourselves as we are and have the desire to love others. Secondly, we have to have a modicum of self-control and be able to handle our hostile impulses, be they jealousy, envy or excessive criticism. Thirdly, we have to be able to recognize the child within us and not let these infantile demands influence our behavior toward others. Not only do we have to control our childish demands but we must also be able to recognize them in other people and not give in to them unless we are willing to be somehow chained or steadily having to gratify them.

To get along with people we must be generous in our judgments of them. We all feel that if people knew the truth behind our lives, they would judge us more kindly. So we must do likewise. The pity is that we expect our friends to live up to the image we have formed of them, a more perfect model than we are able or willing to imitate. No one can have friends unless he can tolerate things which are distasteful to him personally, be able to listen to both sides of an argument and be understanding. Real friendship means and includes understanding, which is that we recognize the worst impulses as well as the best ones of our friends and still like them anyway.

The quickest way to wipe out a friendship is to sponge on it. Moreover, a friend is one who goes around saying nice things about you behind your back and who says nasty things to your face instead of saying them when you are not around. He appreciates your virtues and overlooks your faults, for knowing all about you he likes you just the same. Isn't that just like Jesus taught? Some people seem to spend more time making enemies rather than friendships, but as Abraham Lincoln put it, the best way to destroy enemies is to make them your friends.

One of the major problems in relationships and friendships is the problem of communication. The art of conversation is the art of hearing as well as of being heard. When a friend talks, he wishes to communicate to you his thoughts, feelings, concerns or, simply, some in-

71

formation. You should listen with an open mind — not too open so that it goes in one ear and out the other. Many individuals, instead of listening, are already thinking of what they want to say in rebuttal and are on the defensive. There are few gifts that one person can give to another as rich as understanding. Understanding is an inclination to recognize sympathetically the beliefs of others without necessarily embracing them.

Great people have been good-mannered people and this means having a regard for the other fellow's feelings. The whole secret in making friends is to help them like themselves, by pointing out their good qualities. Shut-ins can do this with anyone that they come in contact with, and they should try to make contact with others by phone, by letter or by an invitation to visit. There is so much you can do for others through a loving friendship by concentrating on being a better friend. Give of yourself as Jesus Christ gives of himself to others: unconditionally. For friendship is the fountain of waters wherein our thirst for love, inspiration, approval and acceptance is quenched.

16

ACCEPTANCE IS . . . FACING REALITY

AS a physician and psychiatrist for many years, I have come to the conclusion that all human beings are handicapped to one extent or another. We are imperfect, either in body or mind and often in both. In our lifetime, we all develop some chronic ailment for which there is no cure. This may range from allergies, arthritis, ulcers or colitis, to more serious disorders such as cardiovascular disease and neurological conditions. Mentally, imperfections that handicap us are personality traits like envy, jealousy, inferiority, violent tempers, anxieties and depression. The list is long, and many of us are blind to these imperfections as we often look at the world "through rose-colored glasses." We only see what we want to see, unable to face reality. It is difficult to accept ourselves as we really are and accepting others as they are. We get disgusted, critical, frustrated or dejected.

Phineas T. Barnum, of circus fame, observed that "a sucker is born every minute" and "every crowd has a silver lining," which accounts for the spate of books and articles that promise happiness, fulfillment and peace of mind. Somehow we cling to the hope that technology and the sacred cow of science will fulfill our hopes and utopian dreams and make us happy, healthy and well-adjusted in a better world. The truth is that the world has never been so unhappy and in such a mess. We have advanced in science to a marvelous degree and declined to the bottom in morality.

An English report on marriage, conducted in a secret survey of a thousand "normal" marriages, revealed that 80% of the respondents, if they had their lives to live over, would marry someone else. Now, this is not a reflection on marriage as much as a reflection that 80% of "normal" people are unhappy, and blame it on the marriage partner rather than on themselves. Unhappiness makes people move to another climate, change jobs or mates, turn to drugs or sex, or even change religions. Few have known that St. Augustine said: "Our hearts are restless, O Lord, until they rest in Thee."

A realist and mystic was the Spanish St. Teresa of Avila, who knew that life was a struggle and peace was death and union with God. She felt that life was merely a long preparation for this death. She also honestly and realistically said that there was not one sin that she had not committed or had thought of committing. An utterly human person, capable of good humor and laughter, she nevertheless had a long life of physical and mental anguish. She suffered a great deal as a young girl during her religious life, with long and painful illnesses, including tuberculosis.

These bouts of illness occurred periodically until her death at age 67 in 1582. St. Teresa remarked: "I was so burning up, so that my nerves began to shrivel and had such unbearable panic that I had no peace day or night, nothing but a deep sadness." It took nearly three years until she recovered enough to be able to crawl on her hands and knees. Bearing her cross of suffering as He did, she surrendered herself completely to God and found ecstasy and rapture in her love for Him.

One of the reasons acceptance is difficult today is that we live in a society of fantasy, a youth-oriented society that glorifies beauty, macho strength and achievement. The emphasis is on independence, and dependence is belittled. Handicaps are treated with indifference, pity and isolation. The sufferings of life are ignored. We do not want to face reality but prefer to escape into an over-idealistic fantasy world. As some wit said, "Life is a continuous process of getting used to things we hadn't expected." But do we ever get used to them?

Shut-ins usually have more than their share of handicaps and less than their share of support from their neighbors. They are vulnerable to self-pity, to fear and anxiety, to loneliness and isolation, to depression. Their increasing dependence increases feelings of bitterness and frustration that, like an acid, corrodes the fibers of their spirit. Revolting against one's infirmities and the natural process of advancing age only serves to bring more suffering and retard any healing. Too many shut-ins live their declining years in passive resignation instead of acceptance of life in its entirety.

Unhappiness often is a state of mind based on a concern for the self. Laid on a foundation of self-centeredness, it is bricked over with self-pity and unacceptance. Acceptance, on the other hand, leads to serenity because we face reality and the truth of life and nature. Shut-ins do not choose to be old or to have afflictions and handicaps. As we all must do, they can only overcome them by accepting them and keeping on living life to the best of their ability. Just as in the marriage vows, we must accept life "for better and for worse." It is all part of God's plan and of the stages of life.

Acceptance means living each day as it comes, according to God's Will and command. We should still be interested in the world about us. St. Paul, in 2 Corinthians 4:16, says: "Though our outer natures are wasting away, our inner nature is being renewed every day." While we cannot do as much as we used to, we can still pray, meditate and love. While we cannot be an "active player" in the game of life, we can still be a spectator and lavish encouragement on others who are still in the game. When St. Teresa surrendered her life to the Will of God, she liberated herself from the world and its false values and became more interested in the Truth, the teachings of Jesus Christ.

Life, after all, is predominantly more of how you take it, rather than of what you make it. Acceptance brings an end to the struggle of life and a more positive motivation toward daily living.

17

THE RAPTURE OF JOY AND HAPPINESS

IN *The Little Flowers of St. Francis of Assisi*, a series of personal stories and accounts preserved by his followers, the tale is told how the saintly ascetic charged a fellow friar that perfect joy is not in the performance of miracles like healing the blind, deaf and crippled, nor in bringing the dead back to life or converting unbelievers to the faith of Christ. When the astonished friar, Brother Leo, asked where perfect joy could be found, St. Francis replied: "When we come to St. Mary of the Angels, soaked by the rain and frozen by the cold, all soiled with mud and suffering from hunger, and we ring at the gate of the place and the brother porter comes and says angrily: 'Who are you?' and we say: 'We are two of your brothers.'

"And he contradicts us, saying: 'You are not telling the truth. Rather you are two rascals who go around deceiving people and stealing what they give to the poor. Go away!' And he does not open for us, but makes us stand outside in the snow and rain, cold and hungry, until night falls. Then if we endure all those insults and cruel rebuffs patiently without being troubled and without complaining, and if we reflect humbly and charitably that the porter really knows us and that God makes him speak against us, oh Brother Leo, write that perfect joy is there!"

Most people think of joy as a sort of emotional "high," followed by some physical activity such as hand-clasping, shouting, leaping, stamping or even breaking into tears. St. Teresa of Avila described her joy as an irresistible rapture, quick sharp shocks in which she felt as though she were being carried upwards and away on eagle wings. Joy has been portrayed as a very glad feeling, delight, ecstasy, rapture, exultation and happiness. Rejoicing means to be full of joy in a high degree to the point of exhilaration. The ancient Hebrews considered joy as an expression of faith in God. The Old Testament relates that when Solomon was anointed and when the House of God was built, "all the people came up after him . . . and rejoiced with great joy . . . and kept the feast of unleavened bread seven days with joy: for the Lord had made them joyful."

In the Declaration of Independence, Thomas Jefferson voiced that every human being had the right to "the pursuit of happiness," and the reason there is so much unhappiness today is that we do not truly know what or how to be happy. To most individuals, "Happiness is. . ." business success, material possessions, status, power, being completely uninhibited or hedonistic. Yet, those who have achieved all these things are still unhappy. Instead they have lost the capacity for joy. While joy is intense and of a briefer duration, happiness is a more moderate feeling and more capable of being sustained longer.

Happiness is not something you can buy or receive as a gift. It comes from doing something worthwhile, in giving of yourself to others. Happiness is attained and preserved by a strong sense of duty and by acquiring self-control or restraint of the passions. It is knowing and believing that God loves us, and that we love others. Just as a child is not happy in getting everything it wants, we should enjoy what we have. The essential elements of holiness are daily efforts to give joy to others, to comfort those in pain, to "throw a little sunshine around," thus happiness and holiness go together.

Maurice Maeterlinck, the Belgian philosopher, said: "It is good to believe that a little more thought, a little more courage, a little more love, a little more curiosity, a little more ardor for living will suffice one day to open for us the gates of joy and truth." Happiness does not come from "doing your own thing," as today's culture seems to emphasize. Rather, this is immaturity at its worst. A truly mature person is one who is content to make others happy without expecting anything in return. His mind is not on himself, but he is attuned to the feelings of others and doing what he is able to bring comfort or help to anyone in need. I remember passing by a little church one day and a sign in front listed the times of services as well as the topic of the coming Sunday's sermon: "What On Earth Are You Doing For Heaven's Sake?" We've all said that at one time in a moment of exasperation, but said slowly it asks a question about our lifestyle. What are we doing with our life for the sake of God in Heaven?

What all this boils down to is that joy and happiness result from being loving, loving yourself because God loves you and loving your fellow-creatures because God loves them too. It takes action on your part. It means going out to those around you. It takes daily effort, concentration, patience, giving, caring and forgiving. It isn't easy to change old habits and attitudes, but if you work at it every day, it gets easier and you will experience a measure of happiness and satisfaction that nothing else will bring.

18

ANYONE CAN BE CREATIVE

THE ability to be creative has always been mysterious and puzzling to those who have tried to unravel the forces that seem to bring something out of nothing. Scientists from all fields and disciplines have come forth with many theories but, alas, they remain just theories. Everything that exists owes its existence to the ultimate Creator, Almighty God. He gave us certain powers to re-create life, as in reproduction, and to use our talents to be creative in the arts, science and other areas of knowledge. While it is true that the world has known many individuals of extraordinary genius and ability, it is also true that all of us have some measure of latent creativity in us that has never been tapped or developed.

Creativity is an act of making, inventing or generating a different look or idea or object that may or may not be original, but is fresh or distinctive. It is a sublimation of our procreative instincts. Women have that ability and feeling when they bring forth a new life that is unique in itself. Men, on the other hand, perhaps being unconsciously envious of this, will create some project and proudly refer to it as: "That's *my* baby!" Ernest Jones, the eminent British psychoanalyst, thought that the spark of genius lay in believing and looking at the world with the fresh and wonderful vision of a child. Children all have a desire to know *why* (that is why they keep asking "why?") and an imagination and curiosity of wonderment.

Creative people possess traits of energy and charm, of ruthlessness and responsibility, being deeply interested in man and his world. They have a greater sensitivity to stimulation of the senses and an unusual capacity for awareness of relationships between various stimuli. They feel deeper and understand more. They are, in a sense, "of this world and in love with it." Sometimes, emotional and neurotic traits have been associated with the creative process. The melancholy moods of Chopin, Tschaikovsky and Sibelius were reflected in their musical works. Artists and poets have often mirrored their feelings of torment in their works. Some have postulated that the creative act is a tension state created by conflict.

Doing something creative is not so much doing something interesting as much as being interested in doing *something*. The work of any of us may matter very little to the world, but it matters very much to ourselves how we do it. Just working at something with enthusiasm gives relish to life and is a perfect escape from self-pity. Turn your imagination loose. All of us are much more creative than we suspect. The housewife who decorates her house with plants, sets a decorative table or does her own interior decorating is expressing herself creatively. Success in creativity is founded on a base of disappointments, failures and fears, as well as achievements.

Everyone has talents of one kind or another and age or handicaps are not barriers to creativity. Besides talent, we need inspiration, imagination and a new way of looking at things. It takes dedication and discipline. We can't give up in frustration at our inadequacies but must continue, practice, learn and enjoy. Robert P. Crawford remarked in *The Techniques of Creative Thinking*: "The tragedy of life is not lack of brain power or education, but doing so little with what we have." Most of us can find originality if we seek it diligently. Creativity can range from "Hints To Heloise" to a pretty design on a ceramic plate.

The inner driving force of imagination and conception should not be kept waiting for a better time or for a flash of inspiration to hit us. We must find something and do it, get down to work on it. Too many people say: "I can't do it" or "I'm not that talented." There never would have been an improvement of any kind at any time if the person with a new idea said: "I can't do it" or "It won't work." All handicapped people, in the course of growing up and adjusting, have learned that "necessity is truly the mother of invention." The woman in the iron lung, because her arms were paralyzed, learned to paint with a brush held between her teeth.

There are many crafts, hobbies and activities that shut-ins can take up, depending on their health and disabilities. Horticulture or raising plants can be enjoyable and creative, both indoors and outdoors. Jewelry-making is another artistic and imaginative hobby that offers an opportunity for creativity with a wide variety of materials and can earn some income. Painting, using watercolors, pastel chalk or acrylic oils, is an artistic endeavor that many retired individuals, including Winston Churchill and Ike Eisenhower, have found to be relaxing and interesting.

One handicapped man got interested in leather work and started making hand-bellows for fireplaces, which turned into a little money-making enterprise. One can get involved in coin-collecting, woodworking, music, knitting, crocheting, reading, writing, decorating and cooking. The list can be endless. Every library has books on hobbies and creative works to challenge one's abilities. Charles Darwin held the opinion, as a result of a lifetime of observation, that people differ less in capacity than in zeal and determination to utilize the talents they have. It is not important to have an "E" for excellence as much as an "E" for effort.

19

DRAWING FROM THE WELL
OF RELIGIOUS STRENGTHS

HISTORY is that branch of knowledge that has recorded the progress and advances of mankind. Man, however, remains unchanged in that he still loves, hopes, fears and is plagued with uncertainty. The passions of the human heart are the same as are the needs for faith and security. It is faith that gives us the fire and strength to work for others and it is the foundation of eternal salvation. We cannot have faith in science because science has never been able to eliminate the destructive forces of nature nor the evil in men's hearts.

The reality of life is that it is temporary for all of us and the truth of life lies in the teachings of Christ in the Bible. Chapter 3 of John tells of how the Pharisee, Nicodemus, came to Jesus one dark night worried that the things that pertained to his everlasting peace were not a part of his prosperous life. Christ's message to him was simply: "With all the earnestness that I possess I tell you this: Unless you are born again, you cannot get into the Kingdom of Heaven."

Jesus went on to explain that anyone who believes in Him will have eternal life and that God did not send His Son into the world to condemn it but to save it. This belief is the essence of faith. In his book *Psychology and Religion*, the late psychoanalyst Carl Jung discussed the beauty and value of religious experience, stating: "If such experience helps to make your life healthier, more beautiful, more complete and more satisfactory to yourself and to those you love, you may safely say: 'This was the grace of God.' No matter what the world thinks about religious experience, the one who has it possesses the great treasure of a thing that has provided him with a source of life, meaning and beauty and that has given a new splendor to the world and to mankind."

It is of the utmost importance while living to have faith. Begin the day with Christ and His prayer, the Lord's Prayer. Learn to know the Bible, because its wisdom still has the power to shape one's character and influence conduct. Reading the Bible for 20 minutes each day and studying its truths will give you fellowship with the great minds of the apostles and prophets, the wisdom of Solomon and the poetry of David. Their words will give you faith, and much can be garnered from their own experiences.

Getting people to love, to be of good faith, to be compassionate and loyal, requires a supernatural effort. Reading and studying the Bible will provide an understanding of the meaning and purpose of why we are created, as well as coping with our personal sufferings. Every Christian bookstore has editions of the Bible that are easy to read and formats on how to make daily reading a part of your life. There are references on various passages that give insight and help with any type of difficulty or problem. It will change your life and bring you that peace that can only come from the Word of God.

20

COMMUNITY AIDS AND SERVICES

SHUT-INS, by virtue of their handicaps, face various problems and difficulties in their daily existence that have to do with finances, home health care, meal preparations, medical care, transporation, security, legal, social and spiritual needs. Every shut-in should be aware of the many aids and services provided directly and indirectly by national, state and local agencies, as well as by many religious charitable organizations and private foundations. While many are listed in the phone directory, every county social service agency has a directory of these services.

The federal government provides no direct help, but funds state, county and city agencies. This includes Medicaid and public welfare assistance. The federal Social Security system provides Supplemental Security income (S.S.I.) to the elderly, disabled or the blind, which also entitles one to Medicaid automatically. Social Security Disability Income (S.S.D.I.) requires that a person must have worked at least 10 quarters to be eligible, and must be disabled, unable to work. Prior approval by one's physician is needed for Medicaid, which offers home-care nursing and a caseworker to assess needs for approval and to develop a care plan, including food shopping, personal care and round-the-clock nursing care when indicated.

The County Directory of Community Services usually lists agencies that cover cultural, educational, health, recreational and social services. If your district has Meals On Wheels, it is listed in the phone book and provides hot meals for those shut-ins who have difficulties with meal preparation. Food stamps, courtesy of the U.S. Department of Agriculture, are obtained from a county division. The county Medicaid system also, with prior approval of one's physician, supplies bus, taxi, wheelchair van and ambulance transportation to and from a hospital, clinic or doctor's office.

As far as security is concerned, most cities have a public service officer in the Police Department who is available for assistance and guidance. Carrier Alert is another security plan wherein a shut-in registers his name and address with police headquarters and the main Post Office. He also gives his phone number and names, addresses and phone numbers of two relatives or friends to contact for the benefit of the shut-in. After this registration, a visible dot is posted inside the shut-in's mailbox. If the mail piles up or the postman notices signs of any kind of trouble, the local police patrolman is called to investigate the situation. He reports to the precinct superior and assistance is provided as needed.

The United Way of America has a Directory of Community Services for each major city and county.

The National Easter Seal Society for Crippled Children and Adults has various programs for aid and service. It is listed in the phone book.

There are many private organizations that deal with

a specific disability, such as the American Heart Association, Arthritis Foundation, National Paraplegia Foundation, American Lung Association, Family of Impairments, National Multiple Sclerosis Society, etc., that offer educational materials, medical guidance and referrals, as well as other forms of assistance.

In most cities, Independent Living Centers have been established. These are usually a coordinating office of professional and volunteer staffs that enable severely disabled persons to live independently. They offer counseling, housing referral and help, attendant coordination and support. The Independent Living Center's programs and services are aimed at promoting independence, productivity and a better quality of life.

Remember that the phone book is an excellent source for listings of these agencies and that hospital, city and county social service departments have workers who will gladly assist you with your needs and problems.